I Can Be a Good Sport

WRITTEN BY ROBIN STANLEY

ILLUSTRATED BY STEVE HARPSTER & TERRY JULIEN

I Can Be a Good Sport copyright © 2006 by Tyndale House Publishers, Inc., Carol Stream, IL 60188. All rights reserved. www.tyndale.com. Originally published as a Happy Day book by Standard Publishing, Cincinnati, Ohio. First printing by Tyndale House Publishers, Inc., in 2015. Scripture quotations are taken from the *Holy Bible*, New Living Translation, copyright © 1996, 2004, 2007, 2013 by Tyndale House Foundation. Used by permission of Tyndale House Publishers, Inc., Carol Stream, Illinois 60188. All rights reserved. *TYNDALE*, Tyndale's quill logo, and *Faith That Sticks* are registered trademarks of Tyndale House Publishers, Inc. For manufacturing information regarding this product, please call 1-800-323-9400.

ISBN 978-1-4964-0309-4

Printed in China

21	20	19	18	17	16	15
7	6	5	4	3	2	1

Tyndale House Publishers, Inc.
Carol Stream, Illinois

I can be a good sport! Being a good sport means trying to be like Jesus all the time! So I'll obey when no one's looking,

hear my coach when he is speaking,

work really hard when I am learning, and be ready
to do my best!

"Whatever you do, do it all
for the glory of God."
1 Corinthians 10:31

I'll be an example to my friends, show them how to be a team.

I won't be selfish with the ball—

The goal's the same for one and all!

When we play together as a team, everyone wins!
Go team!

Love one another and work together
with one heart and purpose.

—*from Philippians 2:2*

I won't cry when I strike out. I did my best, and that's what counts!

If a friend's a little scared of falling on the run, I'll be like Jesus—cheer him on and shout out loud, "Well done!"

I'll keep my cool when I am tempted to really be upset.

And even when we lose the game, I'll shake hands with every player!

"Be humble, thinking of others as better than yourselves."
Philippians 2:3

So, whether I'm an athlete on a team,

or enjoying a family run,

I will choose to be like Jesus, and I'll have a lot more fun!

"Speak the truth in love, growing in every way more and more like Christ. "

Ephesians 4:15

Let's Talk about It

1. How does a good sport behave?

2. When can you be a good sport?

3. How have you acted like a good sport?

4. Who is the best model for good behavior?

5. Why should you be a good sport?

Matching Items

soccer ball

glove

baseball

swimmer

Word Search

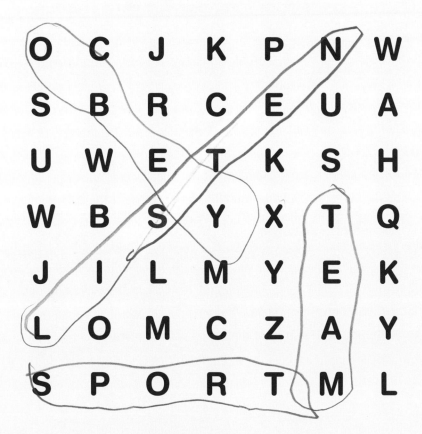

O C J K P N W
S B R C E U A
U W E T K S H
W B S Y X T Q
J I L M Y E K
L O M C Z A Y
S P O R T M L

Find these words

LISTEN • OBEY • SPORT • TEAM

Puzzle made at www.puzzle-maker.com

Craft Activity

Make a pom-pom to cheer for your friends!

Things you will need:

- newspaper
- Popsicle sticks
- tape or rubber bands
- scissors

What to do:

1. Fold a section of newspaper in half.

2. Along the side opposite the fold, cut strips about ½ inch wide, cutting from the loose end toward the fold. Don't cut all the way through the folded edge.

3. Tightly roll up the folded edge of newspaper around the end of a Popsicle stick.

4. Keep the rolled-up newspaper tightly fastened to the Popsicle stick with a rubber band or tape.

5. Rah, rah, sis-boom-bah! Cheer for your friends!

COLORING PAGE

COLORING PAGE

Shape a lifestyle of faith expression in your child —

Our passion is to provide a creative outlet for kids to express their faith in a fun and meaningful way. Cultivate a deeper connection as you teach your child about the impact of God's love, building a legacy of relationship, creativity, and faith to last a lifetime.

Using interactive games, puzzles, and other activities, **Faith That Sticks resources** are a great go-to place for parents who want to teach their kids to love God and to know how much he loves them!

learn more at faiththatsticks.com

More about Reading Levels

PRE-READERS

Books appropriate for pre-readers have

- pictures that reinforce the text
- simple words
- short, simple sentences
- repetition of words and patterns
- large print

BEGINNING READERS

Books appropriate for beginning readers have

- pictures that reinforce the text
- intermediate words
- longer sentences
- simple stories
- dialogue between story characters

INDEPENDENT READERS

Books appropriate for independent readers have

- less need for pictorial support with the text
- more advanced vocabulary
- paragraphs
- longer stories
- more complex subjects

" There are perhaps no days of our childhood we lived so fully as those we spent with a favorite book." — MARCEL PROUST